I ♥ LOVE you

I LOVE YOU

First published in 2014
This edition copyright © Summersdale Publishers Ltd, 2017

Illustrations © Shutterstock

Summersdale Publishers Ltd
46 West Street
Chichester
West Sussex
PO19 1RP
UK

www.summersdale.com

Printed and bound in Croatia

ISBN: 978-1-84953-971-5

Substantial discounts on bulk quantities of Summersdale books are available to corporations, professional associations and other organisations. For details contact general enquiries: telephone: +44 (0) 1243 771107, fax: +44 (0) 1243 786300 or email: enquiries@summersdale.com.

21 years !

Are we matured?
T.

To........................

From........................

Life is the
flower for which
love is the honey.

VICTOR HUGO

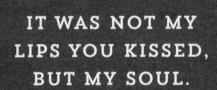

IT WAS NOT MY
LIPS YOU KISSED,
BUT MY SOUL.

JUDY GARLAND

THE WORLD NEEDS MORE LOVE AT FIRST SIGHT.

MAGGIE STIEFVATER

THERE ARE ALL KINDS
OF LOVE IN THIS
WORLD, BUT NEVER THE
SAME LOVE TWICE.

F. SCOTT FITZGERALD

Love is the
STRONGEST
FORCE
the world
possesses.

MAHATMA GANDHI

LOVE IS NOT
CONSOLATION,
IT IS LIGHT.

SIMONE WEIL

She is the heart that strikes a whole octave. After her all songs are possible.

RAINER MARIA RILKE

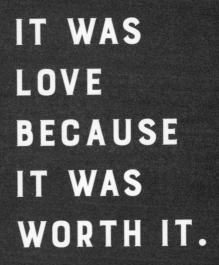

IT WAS
LOVE
BECAUSE
IT WAS
WORTH IT.

JAY ASHER

NO MATTER HOW MANY
SNOWSTORMS WILL PASS
THROUGH YOU, NONE
WILL BRING YOU THE
SPRING LIKE LOVE WILL.

SORIN CERIN

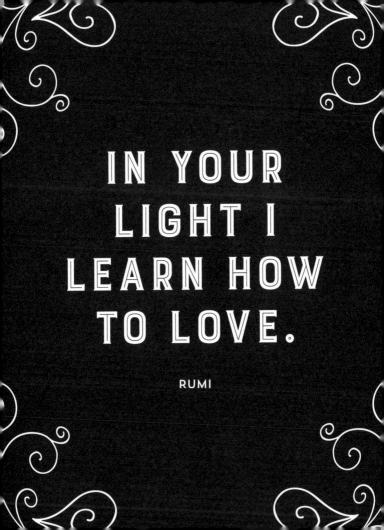

LOVE IS THE
CONDITION IN
WHICH THE
HAPPINESS OF
ANOTHER PERSON
IS ESSENTIAL TO
YOUR OWN.

ROBERT A. HEINLEIN

LOVE HAS NO
UTTERMOST, AS THE
STARS HAVE NO NUMBER
AND THE SEA NO REST.

ELEANOR FARJEON

IF I LOVED YOU
LESS, I MIGHT BE
ABLE TO TALK
ABOUT IT MORE.

JANE AUSTEN

A loving heart
was better and
stronger than wisdom.

CHARLES DICKENS

LOVE IS KEEPING
THE PROMISE
ANYWAY.

JOHN GREEN

Each moment of a happy
lover's hour is worth an age
of dull and common life.

APHRA BEHN

YOURS IS THE LIGHT
BY WHICH MY SPIRIT'S
BORN... YOU ARE MY
SUN, MY MOON, AND
ALL MY STARS.

E. E. CUMMINGS

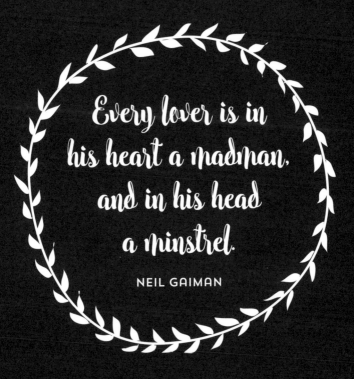

Every lover is in
his heart a madman,
and in his head
a minstrel.

NEIL GAIMAN

LOVE THAT IS NOT MADNESS IS NOT LOVE.

PEDRO CALDERÓN DE LE BARCA

EVENTUALLY, YOU WILL
COME TO UNDERSTAND
THAT LOVE HEALS
EVERYTHING, AND
LOVE IS ALL THERE IS.

GARY ZUKAV

LOVE IS A GAME
THAT TWO CAN PLAY
AND BOTH WIN.

EVA GABOR

If music be the

FOOD OF LOVE,

♡ play on.

WILLIAM SHAKESPEARE

THE BEST THING TO HOLD ONTO IN LIFE IS EACH OTHER.

AUDREY HEPBURN

WHATEVER OUR SOULS
ARE MADE OF, HIS AND
MINE ARE THE SAME.

EMILY BRONTË

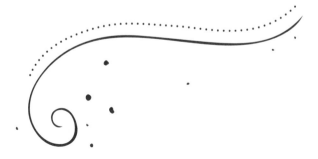

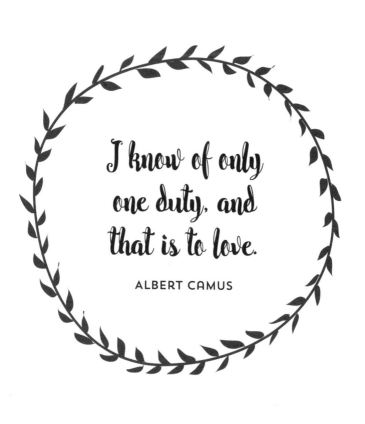

I know of only one duty, and that is to love.

ALBERT CAMUS

I LOVE YOU NOT
ONLY FOR WHAT
YOU ARE, BUT FOR
WHAT I AM WHEN
I AM WITH YOU.

ROY CROFT

IF I HAD A FLOWER
FOR EVERY TIME
I THOUGHT OF
YOU... I COULD
WALK THROUGH MY
GARDEN FOREVER.

ALFRED, LORD TENNYSON

LOVE IS WHAT
MAKES YOU SMILE
WHEN YOU'RE TIRED.

PAULO COELHO

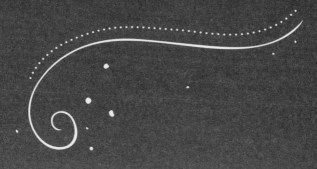

Love unlocks
doors and opens
windows that weren't
even there before.

MIGNON McLAUGHLIN

*If there ever comes a day
when we can't be together,
keep me in your heart.
I'll stay there forever.*

A. A. MILNE

TO LOVE
IS TO RISK
LIVING
FULLY.

LEO BUSCAGLIA

HE IS NOT A LOVER
WHO DOES NOT
LOVE FOREVER.

EURIPIDES

ALL MY HEART IS
YOURS, SIR; IT
BELONGS TO YOU;
AND WITH YOU IT
WOULD REMAIN,
WERE FATE TO
EXILE THE REST
OF ME FROM YOUR
PRESENCE FOREVER.

CHARLOTTE BRONTË

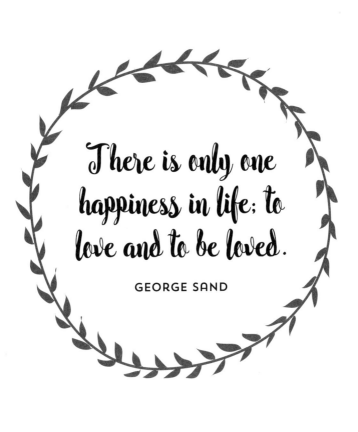

There is only one happiness in life; to love and to be loved.

GEORGE SAND

WHEN YOU FISH FOR LOVE, BAIT WITH YOUR HEART, NOT YOUR BRAIN.

MARK TWAIN

LOVE CONQUERS ALL;
THEREFORE, LET US
SUBMIT TO LOVE.

VIRGIL

TO THE WORLD YOU MAY
BE JUST ONE PERSON,
BUT TO ONE PERSON YOU
MAY BE THE WORLD.

BILL WILSON

IF I WERE TO LIVE
A THOUSAND
YEARS, I WOULD
BELONG TO YOU
FOR ALL OF THEM.

MICHELLE HODKIN

LOVE ISN'T
SOMETHING YOU
FIND. LOVE IS
SOMETHING THAT
FINDS YOU.

LORETTA YOUNG

Love is an

IRRESISTIBLE
DESIRE

to be
irresistibly
desired.

ROBERT FROST

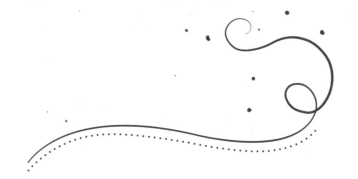

I CRAVE A LOVE SO DEEP THE OCEAN WOULD BE JEALOUS.

ANONYMOUS

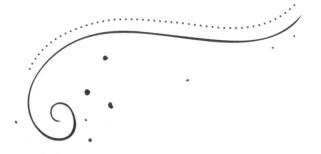

A WOMAN KNOWS
THE FACE OF THE
MAN SHE LOVES AS
A SAILOR KNOWS
THE OPEN SEA.

HONORÉ DE BALZAC

FALLING IN LOVE
COULD BE ACHIEVED
IN A SINGLE
WORD – A GLANCE.

IAN McEWAN

WHEN I FIRST SAW
YOU I FELL IN LOVE,
AND YOU SMILED
BECAUSE YOU KNEW.

ARRIGO BOITO

SOMETIMES THE HEART SEES WHAT IS INVISIBLE TO THE EYE.

H. JACKSON BROWN JR

AND THINK NOT YOU
CAN DIRECT THE COURSE
OF LOVE, FOR LOVE, IF
IT FINDS YOU WORTHY,
DIRECTS YOUR COURSE.

KAHLIL GIBRAN

MY HEART IS AND
ALWAYS WILL
BE YOURS.

JANE AUSTEN

I KNOW BY
EXPERIENCE
THAT THE POETS
ARE RIGHT: LOVE
IS ETERNAL.

E. M. FORSTER

BEING DEEPLY LOVED
BY SOMEONE GIVES
YOU STRENGTH, WHILE
LOVING SOMEONE DEEPLY
GIVES YOU COURAGE.

LAO TZU

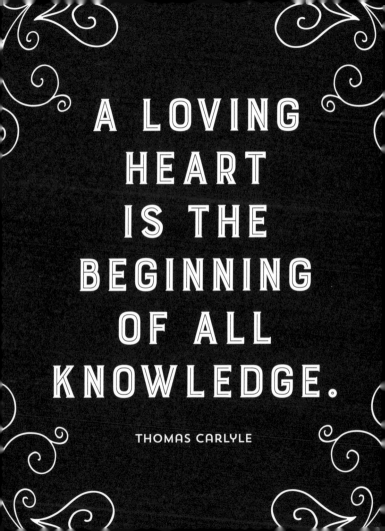

A LOVING
HEART
IS THE
BEGINNING
OF ALL
KNOWLEDGE.

THOMAS CARLYLE

LOVE, LIKE A RIVER, WILL CUT A NEW PATH WHENEVER IT MEETS AN OBSTACLE.

CRYSTAL MIDDLEMAS

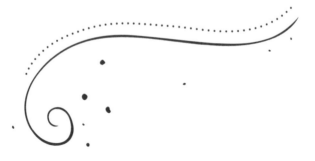

A heart
that loves is
**ALWAYS
YOUNG.**

GREEK PROVERB

KISS ME AND YOU WILL SEE HOW IMPORTANT I AM.

SYLVIA PLATH

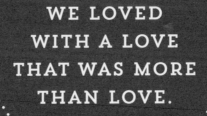

WE LOVED
WITH A LOVE
THAT WAS MORE
THAN LOVE.

EDGAR
ALLAN POE

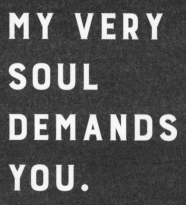

MY VERY SOUL DEMANDS YOU.

CHARLOTTE BRONTË

I love you without knowing how, or when, or from where.

PABLO NERUDA

I FELL IN LOVE THE
WAY YOU FALL ASLEEP:
SLOWLY, AND THEN
ALL AT ONCE.

JOHN GREEN

Love is life.
And if you miss
love, you miss life.

LEO BUSCAGLIA

Come live in
my heart and
pay no rent.

SAMUEL LOVER

AT THE TOUCH OF
LOVE, EVERYONE
BECOMES A POET.

PLATO

I LIKE NOT ONLY TO BE
LOVED, BUT ALSO TO
BE TOLD I AM LOVED.

GEORGE ELIOT

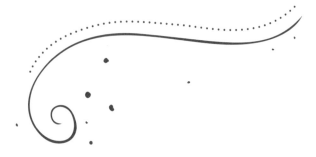

IT IS BEAUTIFUL
TO EXPRESS
LOVE AND EVEN
MORE BEAUTIFUL
TO FEEL IT.

DEJAN STOJANOVIĆ

I DON'T WRITE
POEMS TO MELT
YOUR HEART. I
WRITE THEM, SO
OUR HEARTS CAN
MELT TOGETHER.

SUBHAN ZEIN

KISSES ARE
A BETTER FATE
THAN WISDOM.

E. E. CUMMINGS

There is no remedy for love but to love more.

HENRY DAVID THOREAU

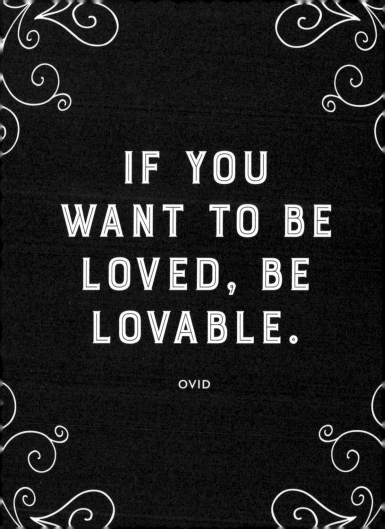

IF YOU
WANT TO BE
LOVED, BE
LOVABLE.

OVID

LOVE IS ALWAYS BEFORE YOU.

ANDRÉ BRETON

I DON'T WANT TO LIVE –
I WANT TO LOVE FIRST,
AND LIVE INCIDENTALLY.

ZELDA FITZGERALD

I SEE YOU
EVERYWHERE, IN
THE STARS, IN
THE RIVER; TO ME
YOU'RE EVERYTHING
THAT EXISTS;
THE REALITY OF
EVERYTHING.

VIRGINIA WOOLF

There is no pretending, I LOVE YOU and I will love you until I die.

CASSANDRA CLARE

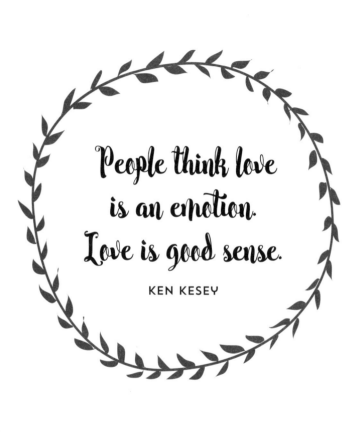

People think love
is an emotion.
Love is good sense.

KEN KESEY

A KISS... IS A ROSY
DOT PLACED ON THE
'I' OF LOVING; 'TIS A
SECRET TOLD TO THE
MOUTH INSTEAD
OF TO THE EAR.

EDMOND ROSTAND

LOVE HAS NO AGE, NO LIMIT; AND NO DEATH.

JOHN GALSWORTHY

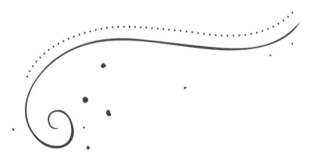

CHOOSE YOUR LOVE, LOVE YOUR CHOICE.

THOMAS S. MONSON

WHAT IS DONE IN
LOVE IS DONE WELL.

VINCENT VAN GOGH

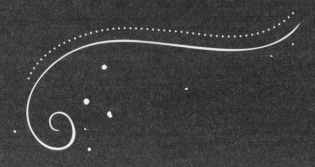

LOVE IS ALL WE
HAVE, THE ONLY
WAY THAT EACH CAN
HELP THE OTHER.

EURIPIDES

LET LOVE STEAL
IN DISGUISED AS
FRIENDSHIP.

OVID

Love is the poetry
of the senses.

HONORÉ DE BALZAC

You should be kissed,
and often, and by someone
who knows how.

MARGARET MITCHELL

LOVE VANQUISHES TIME.

MARY PARRISH

GRAVITATION IS NOT RESPONSIBLE FOR PEOPLE FALLING IN LOVE.

ALBERT EINSTEIN

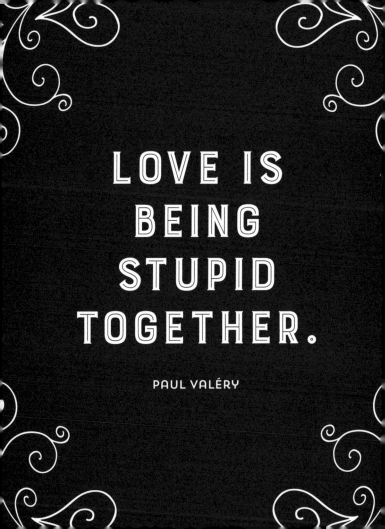

We can only learn
to love by loving.

IRIS MURDOCH

A PART OF KINDNESS CONSISTS IN LOVING PEOPLE MORE THAN THEY DESERVE.

JOSEPH JOUBERT

WHERE THERE IS LOVE THERE IS LIFE.

MAHATMA GANDHI

ONLY DO WHAT YOUR HEART TELLS YOU.

DIANA, PRINCESS OF WALES

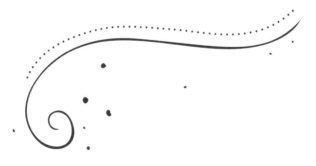

In every living thing there is the desire for love.

D. H. LAWRENCE

Love is a ♡
**SPRINGTIME
PLANET**
that perfumes
everything with
its hope.

GUSTAVE FLAUBERT

Kisses, even to the air, are beautiful.

DREW BARRYMORE

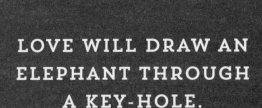

LOVE WILL DRAW AN
ELEPHANT THROUGH
A KEY-HOLE.

SAMUEL RICHARDSON

SOUL
MEETS
SOUL ON
LOVERS'
LIPS.

PERCY BYSSHE SHELLEY

LOVE IS SPACE AND
TIME MEASURED
BY THE HEART.

MARCEL PROUST

TO LOVE BEAUTY
IS TO SEE LIGHT.

VICTOR HUGO

YOU NEVER LOSE BY
LOVING. YOU ALWAYS
LOSE BY HOLDING BACK.

BARBARA DE ANGELIS

FOR SMALL CREATURES
SUCH AS WE THE
VASTNESS IS BEARABLE
ONLY THROUGH LOVE.

CARL SAGAN

*My sort of religion
is one of romance.*

CHRISTOPHER PLUMMER

TO LOVE IS SO
STARTLING IT
LEAVES LITTLE TIME
FOR ANYTHING ELSE.

EMILY DICKINSON

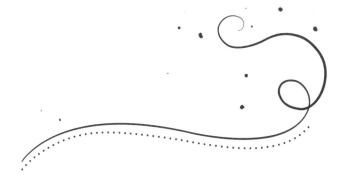

ANYONE CAN BE
PASSIONATE, BUT IT
TAKES REAL LOVERS
TO BE SILLY.

ROSE FRANKEN

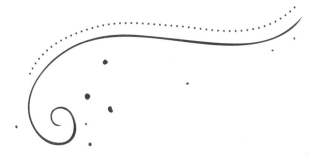

WHAT DOES LOVE FEEL LIKE? INCREDIBLE.

REBECCA ADLINGTON

I carry your heart with me
(I carry it in my heart).

E. E. CUMMINGS

I FEEL THAT THERE IS NOTHING MORE TRULY ARTISTIC THAN TO LOVE PEOPLE.

VINCENT VAN GOGH

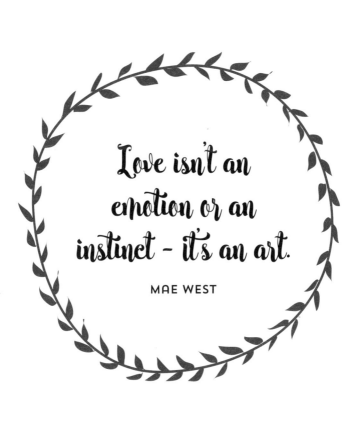

Love isn't an emotion or an instinct – it's an art.

MAE WEST

I have found
that if you

LOVE LIFE,

life will love
you back.

ARTHUR RUBINSTEIN

IGNORANCE AND
BUNGLING WITH
LOVE ARE BETTER
THAN WISDOM AND
SKILL WITHOUT.

HENRY DAVID THOREAU

ALL, EVERYTHING
THAT I UNDERSTAND,
I UNDERSTAND ONLY
BECAUSE I LOVE.

LEO TOLSTOY

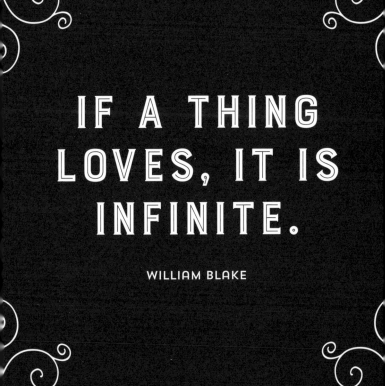

IF A THING LOVES, IT IS INFINITE.

WILLIAM BLAKE

To love is to feel one
being in the world at one
with us, our equal in sin
as well as in virtue.

EMMA ORCZY

I LOVE THAT
FEELING OF BEING
IN LOVE, THE
EFFECT OF HAVING
BUTTERFLIES WHEN
YOU WAKE UP IN
THE MORNING.

JENNIFER ANISTON

YOU MUST ALLOW
ME TO TELL YOU
HOW ARDENTLY
I ADMIRE AND
LOVE YOU.

JANE AUSTEN

THE BEST AND MOST
BEAUTIFUL THINGS...
CANNOT BE SEEN OR EVEN
TOUCHED, BUT MUST BE
FELT WITH THE HEART.

HELEN KELLER

I LOVE YOU THE
SAME WAY I
LEARNED TO RIDE
A BIKE; SCARED
BUT RECKLESS.

RUDY FRANCISCO

LOVE IS A GREAT BEAUTIFIER.

LOUISA MAY ALCOTT

All you need
is love. But a little
chocolate now and
then doesn't hurt.

CHARLES M. SCHULZ

WHERE THERE IS GREAT LOVE THERE ARE ALWAYS MIRACLES.

WILLA CATHER

THEY INVENTED HUGS TO
LET PEOPLE KNOW YOU
LOVE THEM WITHOUT
SAYING ANYTHING.

BIL KEANE

We are
MOST ALIVE
when we're
in love.

JOHN UPDIKE

LOVE IS A BEAUTIFUL DREAM.

WILLIAM SHARP

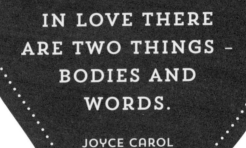

IN LOVE THERE
ARE TWO THINGS –
BODIES AND
WORDS.

JOYCE CAROL
OATES

EACH TIME YOU LOVE, LOVE AS DEEPLY AS IF IT WERE FOREVER.

AUDRE LORDE

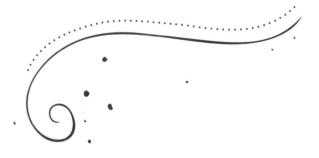

Respect is what
we owe; love,
what we give.

PHILIP JAMES BAILEY

SPEAK LOW, IF YOU SPEAK LOVE.

WILLIAM SHAKESPEARE

LOVE IS LIKE PI –
NATURAL, IRRATIONAL,
AND VERY IMPORTANT.

LISA HOFFMAN

WE CAN'T COMMAND
OUR LOVE, BUT WE
CAN OUR ACTIONS.

ARTHUR CONAN DOYLE

Because of a great love, one is courageous.

LAO TZU

LOVE WILL FIND A WAY
THROUGH PATHS WHERE
WOLVES FEAR TO PREY.

LORD BYRON

LIFE IN ABUNDANCE
COMES ONLY
THROUGH
GREAT LOVE.

ELBERT HUBBARD

*You are always new,
the last of your kisses
was ever the sweetest.*

JOHN KEATS

MAY WE SO LOVE
AS NEVER TO
HAVE OCCASION
TO REPENT OF
OUR LOVE.

HENRY DAVID THOREAU

YOU KNOW YOU'RE
IN LOVE WHEN YOU
CAN'T FALL ASLEEP
BECAUSE REALITY
IS FINALLY BETTER
THAN YOUR DREAMS.

ANONYMOUS

Love is the greatest refreshment in life.

PABLO PICASSO

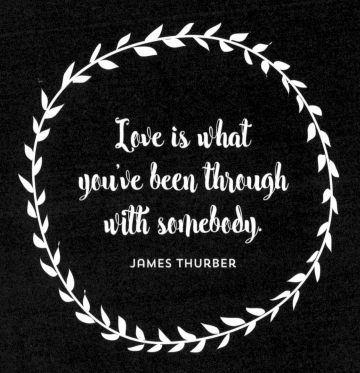

Love is what
you've been through
with somebody.

JAMES THURBER

A KISS IS A LOVELY
TRICK DESIGNED BY
NATURE TO STOP
WORDS WHEN SPEECH
BECOMES SUPERFLUOUS.

INGRID BERGMAN

WE LOVE BECAUSE IT IS THE ONLY TRUE ADVENTURE.

NIKKI GIOVANNI

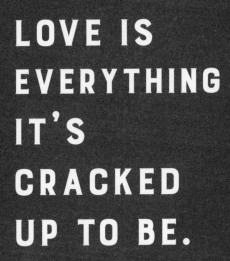

LOVE IS EVERYTHING IT'S CRACKED UP TO BE.

ERICA JONG

IN ART AS IN
LOVE, INSTINCT
IS ENOUGH.

ANATOLE FRANCE

THUS LOVE HAS
THE MAGIC POWER
TO MAKE OF A
BEGGAR A KING.

EMMA GOLDMAN

WHAT THE WORLD
REALLY NEEDS IS
MORE LOVE AND
LESS PAPERWORK.

PEARL BAILEY

LOVE IS COMPOSED
OF A SINGLE
SOUL INHABITING
TWO BODIES.

ARISTOTLE

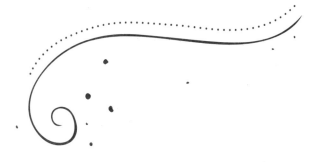

I CAN LIVE WITHOUT
MONEY, BUT I CANNOT
LIVE WITHOUT LOVE.

JUDY GARLAND

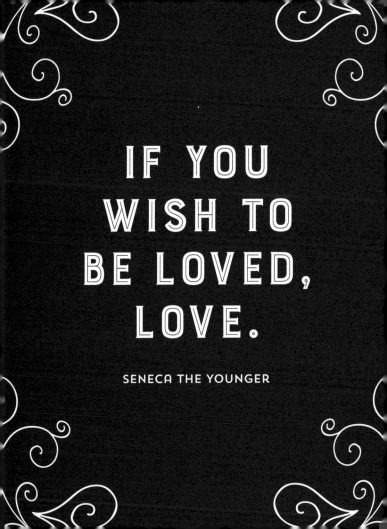

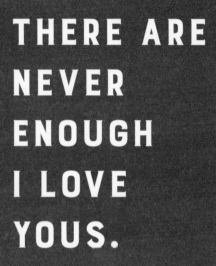

THERE ARE
NEVER
ENOUGH
I LOVE
YOUS.

LENNY BRUCE

Love is not only something you feel, it is

SOMETHING YOU DO.

DAVID WILKERSON

TO LOVE AND BE LOVED
IS TO FEEL THE SUN
FROM BOTH SIDES.

DAVID VISCOTT

DO YOU HAVE TO HAVE A REASON FOR LOVING?

BRIGITTE BARDOT

THE MADNESS OF LOVE IS THE GREATEST OF HEAVEN'S BLESSINGS.

PLATO

What is love?... It is the morning star and it is also the evening star.

SINCLAIR LEWIS

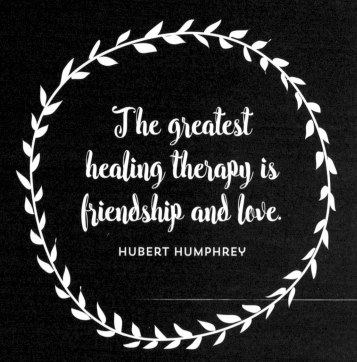

The greatest healing therapy is friendship and love.

HUBERT HUMPHREY

ESKIMOS HAD
FIFTY-TWO NAMES
FOR SNOW BECAUSE
IT WAS IMPORTANT TO
THEM: THERE OUGHT TO
BE AS MANY FOR LOVE.

MARGARET ATWOOD

LOVE IS FRIENDSHIP SET ON FIRE.

JEREMY TAYLOR

IF YOU DON'T LOVE ME,
IT DOES NOT MATTER,
ANYWAY I CAN LOVE
FOR BOTH OF US.

STENDHAL

TRUE LOVE
DOESN'T COME TO
YOU, IT HAS TO
BE INSIDE YOU.

JULIA ROBERTS

Love is the
RIVER
OF LIFE
in the
world.

HENRY WARD BEECHER

WHEN THE HEART
SPEAKS, HOWEVER
SIMPLE THE WORDS,
ITS LANGUAGE IS
ALWAYS ACCEPTABLE
TO THOSE WHO
HAVE HEARTS.

MARY BAKER EDDY

TO LOVE IS TO WILL THE GOOD OF THE OTHER.

THOMAS AQUINAS

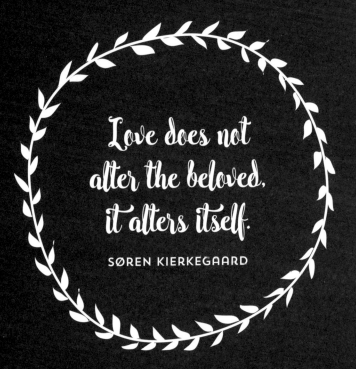

Love does not
alter the beloved,
it alters itself.

SØREN KIERKEGAARD

ULTIMATELY, LOVE
IS EVERYTHING.

M. SCOTT PECK

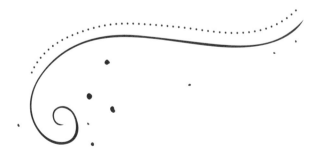

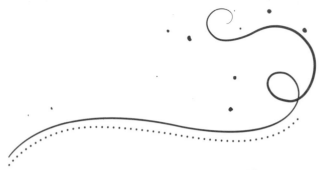

IF YOU'RE INTERESTED IN
FINDING OUT MORE ABOUT OUR
BOOKS, FIND US ON FACEBOOK
AT SUMMERSDALE PUBLISHERS
AND FOLLOW US ON
TWITTER AT @SUMMERSDALE.

WWW.SUMMERSDALE.COM

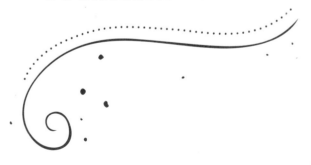